MONSTERS

BY

J.M. SERTORI

WHAT IS A MONSTER?

Why do we feel the need to be afraid? Monsters are born out of the dark, out of the unknown, out of the things that human beings don't fully understand. Our ancestors' fears were often justified, and deep in all our souls there still lives a cave-dweller, ever-fearful of wild animals, ever-worried about where the next meal will come from, ever-terrified of the dark, of thunder, lightning, loneliness, and desertion. Such instinctive fears make us all too willing to believe in monsters. Even today, many people continue to be afraid of the dark because it represents the unknown. With the lights off, our eyes fail us, our other senses can become confused or even desert us. The human mind fills in gaps, jumps to conclusions and often creates monsters out of nothing but its own fears.

PRIMAL FOREST

Forests can be dark forbidding places, home to unknown creatures and easy to get lost in. For our ancestors, who lived before the days of convenient paths and rest-stops, the forest hid enemy attackers and savage predators. Perhaps worst of all was the fear of having an accident and never being found by friends or relatives. Those who wander off the beaten track do so at their peril. 'Whatever you do,' say wise adults in fairy stories, 'don't go into the forest.' On the way to her granny's house Red Riding Hood forgot to heed her mother's warning and very nearly became a wicked wolf's dinner.

TOOTH & CLAW

This cat is displaying its fangs because it is scared or angry, but the message it sends to the viewer is that it is not a creature to be messed with. Deep down inside us all there is a creature who responds to danger signals such as bared fangs, and whose instinct to run away remains almost irresistible. Fear is our natural safeguard and the impulse to run has saved many lives.

THINGS THAT SHOULD NOT BE

Generation after generation add to the myths and stories of dragons, werewolves, vampires, and devils. Eventually, so many stories are told that they take on a life of their own. This creature is obviously a dragon but it has been created by human hands. Many of the monsters that scare us are very human inventions.

NIGHTMARES

When we sleep and our brain goes into neutral gear, random thoughts and things we try not to think about can sometimes bump together to produce nightmares. This picture, *The Nightmare* by Fuseli, combines fears of the dark and the unknown.

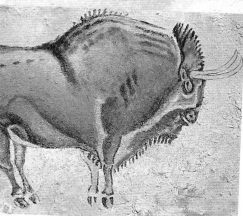

CAVE PAINTINGS

Before there was any other means of recording information, our ancestors painted pictures on the walls of their caves. Like all art, the pictures reflected the hopes, dreams, and fears of their creators. This great bison was probably part of a wish-list addressed to the gods. By drawing or symbolizing it on the wall its creator may have hoped to control his or her fear of a more powerful beast. This may explain our own enthusiasm for horror stories. Talking about, or giving a visible form to what scares us can help to make it less scary.

 FOOD FOR THOUGHT

Monsters do not exist. However, we use them to represent our worst fears and by confronting them we may help ourselves to overcome them. While monsters are not real, our fears certainly are. There might just be something at the window, or sneaking up behind you. There is danger in the woods! There is violence in the world. It is wise to keep your fear instinct well tuned. Dragons do not exist, but dinosaurs did, and crocodiles still do! Sometimes, fact really is stranger and scarier than fiction.

NATURAL MONSTERS

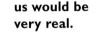

Not all monsters are figments of the human imagination. Perhaps the most fearsome creatures to have lived were the dinosaurs. Fortunately, these prehistoric monsters never shared the Earth with us; they died out some 65 million years ago, long before we arrived. But the natural world still has plenty of other fierce creatures to inspire a sense of the monstrous in mankind. The ancestry of some, such as crocodiles, can be traced back to the Mesozoic Era when dinosaurs lived. Were we to encounter these creatures roaming free in their natural habitat, the potential dangers facing us would be very real.

KILLER FISH

The piranha school is another monstrous fear. A single fish is ugly but relatively harmless. An entire school of these sharp-toothed creatures can strip the flesh from a creature in the water within seconds. In Brazil in 1981, more than 300 people were eaten alive by piranhas when a boat capsized near Obidos.

TYRANNOSAURUS REX

The most famous of the dinosaurs, this gargantuan, meat-eating predator was genuinely fearsome. Up to 14.5 metres (47 ft) long and 6 metres (20 ft) high, it weighed almost 8 tons and boasted fangs 15 cm (6 inches) long. These awesome creatures terrorized East Asia and North America but, luckily for us, the last tyrannosaur died millions of years before the arrival of humanity.

FOOD FOR THOUGHT

Are there real-life mammoths in Siberia? The 'evidence' has probably come from dead mammoths only recently dug out of ancient ice. In the thirteenth century, Genghis Khan turned a herd of elephants loose on the Russian steppes. It is unlikely that any of their descendants live undiscovered today, and even less likely is the survival of mammoths! The way all these creatures are so different to us makes us see them as monstrous. Their teeth, their savage speed, their reptilian origins, all scare us, but they are not monsters. Lions only hunt for food; the crocodile has no interest in human affairs; and no tyrannosaur ever declared war or committed a crime. Only humans have fought to master the natural world. As part of nature, perhaps our greatest fear is that by harming its creatures we may one day harm ourselves.

MAMMOTHS

Elephants are large and scary enough. Imagine if they had extra long tusks and were hairy. The bodies of prehistoric mammoths have been found in the ice of Siberia and the local tribesmen have been known to take the tusks to sell as ivory. Some people in remote parts of Russia have reported seeing live mammoths but their stories are difficult to substantiate.

THE KING CHEETAH

Thought for many years to be nothing more than a ghost story, this huge predator with a tiger-like stripe down its back has been known to carry off people along the Mozambique border. Called a *mngwa* by the locals, rumours of its existence were proved true when Paul and Lena Bottriel photographed the 'king' cheetah in 1975.

CROCODILE TEARS

Around 2,000 people a year fall prey to salt-water crocodiles. Left over from prehistory, crocodiles have been hunting by the riverside for eons. They are not natural enemies of man because, in fact, they have been around far longer than the human race. If we invade their natural habitat it is our own fault if they attack us, yet we have demonized these creatures.

THE LION'S SHARE

Today, lions and tigers are familiar to us from television and zoos. But in the wild, before the days of guns and traps, these big cats were greatly feared. Wise humans left them well alone, even though a lion would only attack a human being if it was provoked. Like many so-called *monsters* of the world, they are more likely to be afraid of us than we are of them.

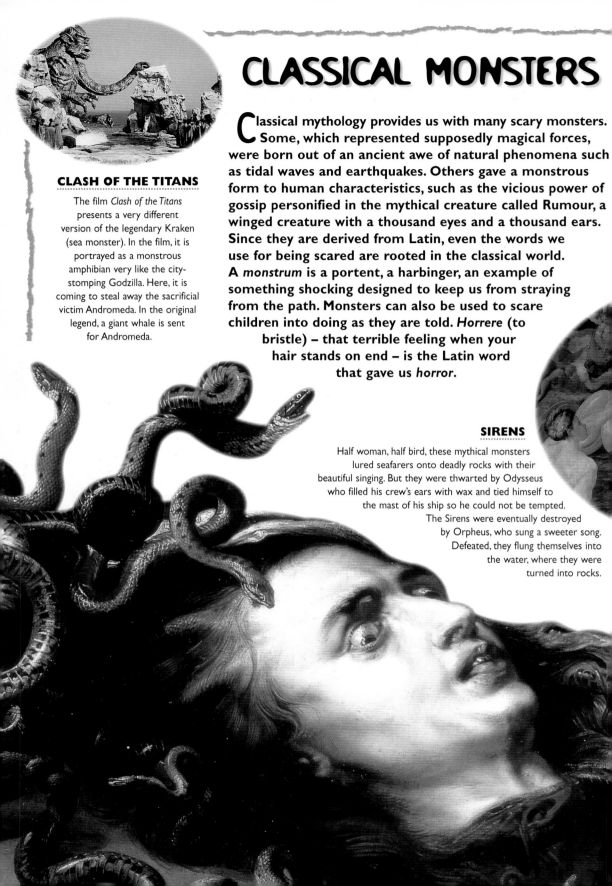

CLASSICAL MONSTERS

CLASH OF THE TITANS

The film *Clash of the Titans* presents a very different version of the legendary Kraken (sea monster). In the film, it is portrayed as a monstrous amphibian very like the city-stomping Godzilla. Here, it is coming to steal away the sacrificial victim Andromeda. In the original legend, a giant whale is sent for Andromeda.

Classical mythology provides us with many scary monsters. Some, which represented supposedly magical forces, were born out of an ancient awe of natural phenomena such as tidal waves and earthquakes. Others gave a monstrous form to human characteristics, such as the vicious power of gossip personified in the mythical creature called Rumour, a winged creature with a thousand eyes and a thousand ears. Since they are derived from Latin, even the words we use for being scared are rooted in the classical world. A *monstrum* is a portent, a harbinger, an example of something shocking designed to keep us from straying from the path. Monsters can also be used to scare children into doing as they are told. *Horrere* (to bristle) – that terrible feeling when your hair stands on end – is the Latin word that gave us *horror*.

SIRENS

Half woman, half bird, these mythical monsters lured seafarers onto deadly rocks with their beautiful singing. But they were thwarted by Odysseus who filled his crew's ears with wax and tied himself to the mast of his ship so he could not be tempted. The Sirens were eventually destroyed by Orpheus, who sung a sweeter song. Defeated, they flung themselves into the water, where they were turned into rocks.

THE MINOTAUR

A man with the head of a bull – supposedly the result of a curse on Minos, the King of Crete – the minotaur lived in the centre of a great maze. Each year, the Athenians had to send seven boys and seven girls to be sacrificed to the minotaur, or risk invasion. The minotaur was eventually slain by Theseus, a Greek hero who went in disguise as one of the sacrificial victims. Theseus fell in love with Ariadne, the daughter of the King of Crete, who gave him a sword and a roll of string by which he could retrace his steps through the maze.

HYDRA

The hero Hercules was told to defeat the hydra, a snake-like monster with nine heads. Each time he struck off one of the heads with his club, two more would grow in its place. But Hercules managed to burn away eight of the heads before burying the ninth (which was immortal) under a rock.

MEDUSA

The Gorgons were three terrifying creatures who had snakes instead of hair, as well as wings, claws, and enormous teeth. Two of them, Stheno and Euryale, were immortal, but the most famous was the mortal Medusa. Once a beautiful girl, she was turned into a monster by the jealous Greek goddess, Athena. Medusa became so ugly that one look at her face would turn men into stone. The hero Perseus defeated her by looking only at her reflection. He was then able to cut off her head. But even after death, the sight of her ugliness continued to petrify anyone who looked upon her.

FOOD FOR THOUGHT

Superstition and religion were the science of the ancient world. But these stories, the entertainments of the times, were often rooted in real events. The people of Crete worshipped a bull-god. Perhaps this, coupled with fear of invasion, was muddled over time to become the tale of the minotaur. The story of the Sirens contains its own explanation. The Sirens were dangerous rocks and the story warned sailors of their presence. And what's worse than a snake? A snake with ten heads, of course! How ugly is the ugliest person you can think of? So ugly you'd die if you looked at them!

DRAGONS

The dragon is the super-monster of many cultures, and is born of a mixture of many different creatures. The Chinese legend of the birth of the dragon was that as tribes with different animal totems united they produced a composite creature with the antlers of a deer, the body of a snake, the wings of a bird (and so on). Eventually, they had invented a creature like no earthly beast. In Chinese, the word *dragon* is also used to describe waterspouts and tornadoes, which reinforces the idea of a dragon as an unstoppable force of nature. The American Indians created their own equivalent in their Thunder Lizard legends, inspired by their discovery of dinosaur bones – they could not have known that these creatures had been dead for millions of years. Once again, these are examples of the human mind fleshing out monsters created largely in the imagination.

SNAKES IN THE GRASS

The serpent is a symbol of evil in many cultures. See the forked tongue, a symbol of telling lies, and hence of evil and deception.

THE EVIL SERPENT

Western dragons have their origins in the Greek *drakon* meaning *serpent*. More likely to be dangerous (Chinese dragons are just tough), Western dragons have become the personification of evil and of the Devil himself (notably, the Serpent in the Garden of Eden). Here, Saint George defeats 'the dragon'. Some other pictures depict the dragon as a human figure.

 FOOD FOR THOUGHT

Until causes are understood, humankind creates monsters to explain fearful events such as tornadoes, waterspouts and earthquakes. The Komodo Dragon is called a dragon, yet it doesn't fly nor breathe fire. If you call a pet hamster Dragon, it doesn't make him one.

EARTHQUAKES

On the rare occasions in the past when our ancestors found dinosaur fossils, they did not know how to explain them. Some assumed that the bones were of giant creatures who lived in the bowels of the earth. When one of the sleeping giants shivered, the whole earth would quake.

THUNDER & LIGHTNING

In China, the word for *dragon* was also used to describe thunder and lightning flashing in the sky. This helps to explain the longer, snakelike shape of the oriental dragon. To an ancient Chinese sage, this picture would show two dragons fighting in the sky. Storms weren't the only natural phenomena attributed to the work of dragons, however. Offshore tornadoes that whisked water into great whirling spouts were known as sea dragons. This meant that matter-of-fact reports of bad weather could have been misunderstood as attacks by supernatural creatures.

ORIENTAL DRAGONS

East Asian dragons are normally good-natured. As long as they are respected, they can act with great kindness. According to some stories, a great person may become an immortal or a spirit. After many centuries, the spirit becomes a dragonet and dives beneath the earth to sleep. When it finally wakes as a dragon, it tears itself free and flies up to heaven.

A REAL DRAGON

In 1912, a 3-metre (10-ft) lizard that ate pigs and goats was discovered in the islands of the Indian Ocean. It was immediately dubbed the Komodo dragon, as it is still called today. In 1979, an expedition to New Guinea found archaeological evidence of an even bigger lizard. Perhaps a live specimen is still waiting to be discovered.

SCARING YOUR ENEMIES

This suit of Japanese samurai armour is designed to look monstrous. In the heat of battle, warriors needed all the help they could get. Horned helmets or even spiked armour for their horses all helped to terrify their enemies.

GRENDEL

In the Old English epic tale of *Beowulf*, Grendel was the troll-like creature who plagued King Hrothgar's hall for twelve years. Eventually, Grendel was slain by Beowulf, the hero who wrestled with him and tore off his arm. Grendel's mother came seeking vengeance for her son and proved to be an even more dangerous foe.

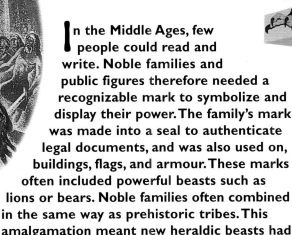

FAMILY FORTUNES

In the Middle Ages, few people could read and write. Noble families and public figures therefore needed a recognizable mark to symbolize and display their power. The family's mark was made into a seal to authenticate legal documents, and was also used on, buildings, flags, and armour. These marks often included powerful beasts such as lions or bears. Noble families often combined in the same way as prehistoric tribes. This amalgamation meant new heraldic beasts had to be created that included different parts from each family's coat of arms. These new non-existent creatures became symbols of the larger more powerful family.

GRIFFIN

The Griffin is part eagle, part lion. These two heraldic symbols are a sign of power and strength – and combined they make a scary monster indeed. A remarkably similar idea of something superpowerful is found in Chinese culture – a tiger with wings.

HERALDIC BEASTS

Noble families often regarded their family symbols as guardian spirits, or designed them to strike fear into their enemies.

CHIMAERA

In Greek mythology, this fire-breathing monster had the hind parts of a dragon, the body of a goat, the forelegs of a lion, and the heads of all three. A fearsome creature, yet its origin can be traced to the geography around the Chimaera volcano in Lycia, an ancient region on the coast of S.W. Asia Minor. It had a fiery summit, lions in its upper forests, goats on the lower slopes, and serpents in the marshes at its foot.

 FOOD FOR THOUGHT

Was Grendel a real person? Probably not, but as a symbol of an enemy tribe he must have seemed a fearsome foe. Many of these heraldic monsters are symbols of synergy, of the power gained through cooperation with others.

They embody the challenge, 'You and whose army?', a clear threat to your enemies that if they cross you, they also cross your allies. The concept of mixed breeds still scares us. Just look at the modern-day horror story of The Fly in which a laboratory accident forces a man and a fly to become one fearsome creature. Modern-day horror tales of genetic mutation and experiments continue to inspire monstrous tales.

FROM DJINNI TO GENIE

Middle Eastern *djin* (demons) were thought to have been created from fire 2,000 years before Adam was made out of clay. They entered Western mythology as genies, although their original destructive powers have been tempered over time to offer little more than the granting of wishes.

 **FOOD FOR THOUGHT**

Some real people are born small – the average height of the Congo Mbutsi tribe is a mere 137 cm (4 ft 6 in) – but they have no relation to the mythical beings shown here. It is said that elves and fairies are wounded by iron. This may refer to the local peoples of Bronze Age culture being pushed into the forests and wilderness by invading Iron Age tribes. Other fairy tales seem to be remnants of pagan religions, belittled by the arrival of Christianity and mutated as they were passed by word of mouth through the generations.

Ultimately, the simplest explanation works best – if you can't think of a good reason for some act of mischief, blame an evil spirit. Of course, mischief-makers have to be small; if they were giants, everyone else would have seen them, too. The sound of mice scurrying behind the walls may have added credence to the ancient legends.

GOBLINS, KOBOLDS & SPIRITS

Perhaps with their origins in the desire of children to have something smaller than themselves in the world, the little people are another kind of monster. Sometimes demonic, they are more often impudent or mischievous rogues who dwell in our houses, chinks in trees, and other nooks and crannies. The mythologies of most cultures include stories of little people such as gnomes, goblins, kobolds, and leprechauns. They were often portrayed as misshapen old men

who hoarded treasure. The most famous are perhaps the Scandinavian Norse dwarves. They had their own king, were not unfriendly to humans, but could be very vindictive or mischievous. The Norse word *alfar* may have given us the English word *elf*.

DWARVES

According to Norse mythology, dwarves began their existence as maggots in the flesh of a giant. Found in the mythology of most races, they were said to live beneath the earth, or in rocks, and to be guardians of its precious metals and stones. Dwarves were sometimes believed to help human beings. Carved on this stone tomb, four dwarves are depicted supporting the sky over a dead Viking.

KOBOLDS

Another kind of dwarf said to live in German mines, Kobolds did everything they could to make life difficult for silver miners. They would cause cave-ins, explosions, and rockfalls. Miners lived in dread of their activities. Sometimes, they mixed silver ore with their own magic metal and this became known as *cobalt*.

FAIRIES

We think of fairies as the tiny butterfly-like creatures we know from Victorian children's stories. But in earlier times they were something to be afraid of – marauding creatures said to steal babies from their mothers' arms. Fairies began as denizens of the dark forests, creatures who would lure unsuspecting travellers to their doom. In the Middle Ages, they were symbols of temptation; they lured people to commit sin without revealing that there would be a horrible price to pay.

ELVES

Although sometimes allies of humans, elves were notoriously unreliable, always likely to go back on bargains and twist the words of promises. In the Middle Ages when a child was born dead or disabled it was believed that fairies or elves had swapped the human child for one of their own – a changeling. It is often said that elves are hurt by iron, a metal said in China to 'wound the eyes of dragons'.

FOOD FOR THOUGHT

There is an element of truth in these stories. Some people do grow to be very tall, but that doesn't make them monsters. Tall people often suffer from a variety of ailments, including bad backs, stoops, and tunnel vision. The latter may explain why Goliath did not notice a rock flying at him from the side. But what about the really big giants of legend? Many are folktales that grew out of the need to explain strange natural phenomena. Most, as usual, are products of the human mind. In the earliest days of childhood, we are loomed over by adults so much taller than we are that to a tiny child they could seem like giants.

GOLIATH

A huge champion of the Philistines in the Bible, Goliath was defeated by a stone slung at him by David, the future King of Israel. He was said to stand 2.75 metres (9 ft) high or, according to another source, 1.8 metres (6 ft) high – the difference between a tall story and a tall man.

REAL-LIFE GIANTS

In Kashmir, two towering men stand on either side of a tiny Professor Ricalton, but how *giant* are they? Perhaps the professor is actually quite short – the 'giants' are much taller than average but not excessively so. People of great height are not unheard of but the picture is oddly posed. Professor Ricalton has taken his hat off; while the two 'giants' wear turbans that make them look taller. The image is impressive, but parts of it are cosmetic – rather like a puffer fish that pretends to be bigger than it is. Great size or the illusion of it is used in the natural world to scare away potential predators.

GIANTS

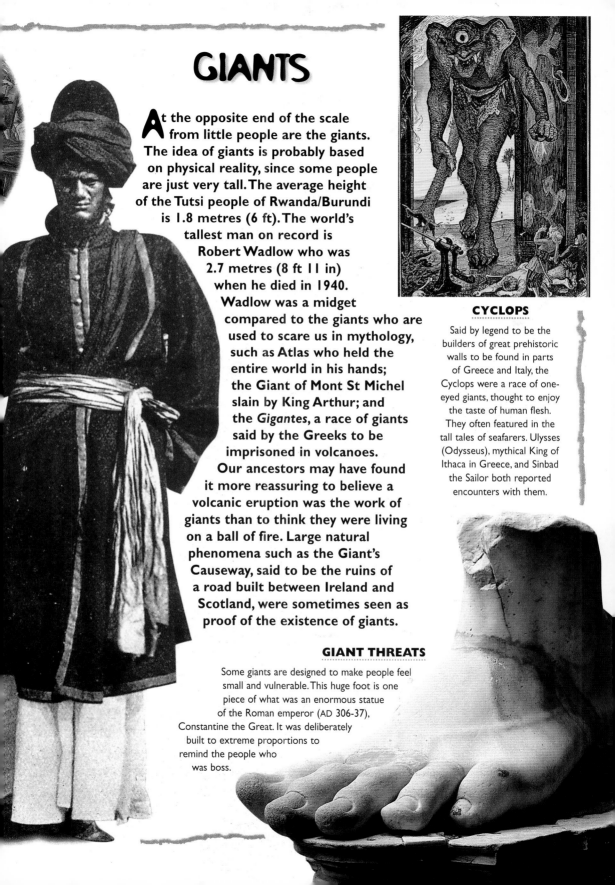

At the opposite end of the scale from little people are the giants. The idea of giants is probably based on physical reality, since some people are just very tall. The average height of the Tutsi people of Rwanda/Burundi is 1.8 metres (6 ft). The world's tallest man on record is Robert Wadlow who was 2.7 metres (8 ft 11 in) when he died in 1940. Wadlow was a midget compared to the giants who are used to scare us in mythology, such as Atlas who held the entire world in his hands; the Giant of Mont St Michel slain by King Arthur; and the *Gigantes*, a race of giants said by the Greeks to be imprisoned in volcanoes.

Our ancestors may have found it more reassuring to believe a volcanic eruption was the work of giants than to think they were living on a ball of fire. Large natural phenomena such as the Giant's Causeway, said to be the ruins of a road built between Ireland and Scotland, were sometimes seen as proof of the existence of giants.

CYCLOPS

Said by legend to be the builders of great prehistoric walls to be found in parts of Greece and Italy, the Cyclops were a race of one-eyed giants, thought to enjoy the taste of human flesh. They often featured in the tall tales of seafarers. Ulysses (Odysseus), mythical King of Ithaca in Greece, and Sinbad the Sailor both reported encounters with them.

GIANT THREATS

Some giants are designed to make people feel small and vulnerable. This huge foot is one piece of what was an enormous statue of the Roman emperor (AD 306-37), Constantine the Great. It was deliberately built to extreme proportions to remind the people who was boss.

VAMPIRES

 FOOD FOR THOUGHT

The idea of vampires is really fairly silly, but they do combine several important elements. There's the historical aspect, and the fear of a powerful individual who abuses those less fortunate than himself. But, ultimately, vampire stories are rooted in a fear of the dead and in the observation of what happens after people die. Their skin shrinks back slightly, making teeth and nails look longer; they become pale as if their blood has been drained away. A wolf or a bat is just an animal, but say it's possessed by a dead soul and you have a scary story. And a cloud of gas! Might this be methane gas rising over a graveyard from a decaying body beneath the earth? There's a rational explanation for everything except perhaps why people find these stories so compelling.

S upposedly the ghost of a heretic (a person who holds different beliefs to those of the established church) or a criminal, a vampire comes out of its grave at night in the guise of a bat to suck blood from people as they sleep. As a result, the victims become vampires. The most famous vampire is from the novel *Dracula* (1897) by Bram Stoker. Count Dracula was based on two historical figures but legends of vampirism existed long before the book was written. Some myths say vampires cannot be reflected in a mirror because they have no soul. Also, old mirrors were made with silver and, since Jesus was betrayed for 30 pieces, silver was thought to reflect evil.

ACULA HAS RISEN FROM THE GRAVE

IER LEE

VERONICA CARLSON · BARBARA EWING · BARRY ANDREWS · EWAN HOOPER

MODERN VAMPIRES

Modern myths say vampires can change into wolves, bats, or even clouds of gas. They have long fangs for sinking into human flesh and drinking blood, and they have to stay out of sunlight. They can only be killed by a stake through the heart.

VLAD THE IMPALER

Vlad V of Walachia (1456-1476) was born in 1431 in Transylvania. He was a brutal warlord reputed to have killed over a hundred thousand people. Stories tell of him nailing hats to people's heads, skinning them alive and, most famously, impaling them on upright stakes – for which he earned the nickname Vlad the Impaler. He was also called Vlad, son of the dragon (or Dracula). His behaviour made some people think he had sold his soul to the devil, and led to rumours that he would never be admitted into heaven. Murdered in 1476, his tomb was reported empty, and the legends began.

THE VAMPIRE BAT

This humble bat scrapes a hole in an animal's skin and drinks its blood. In that sense, it is little different from a mosquito (just bigger), but the blood-drinking was associated with vampirism and the name stuck.

WERE-CREATURES

A true were-creature is half man, half beast. From early prehistoric cave paintings we can see that primitive shaman were thought to have the power of shape-shifting. Similar stories were told of the Vikings, who often wore wolf skins to strike fear into their enemies. In modern mythology, such as the film *I Was a Teenage Werewolf*, werewolves have been given an additional dimension: the teenager boy's monstrous fear of never being loved, of having a dark side that cannot be tamed, of being a rebel without a cause, or a beast in search of a beauty to tame him.

THE FULL MOON

Werewolves supposedly take on their beastly shape at the full moon, when supernatural powers are at their greatest.

FOOD FOR THOUGHT

The idea of changing into a wolf (or in some cultures into tigers, bears, or lions) shows a natural human fear of the monstrous. It symbolizes leaving the safety of civilization and plunging back into the past to become the very thing our ancestors sought to hide from – our own animal nature. As with the shape-shifting vampire, some people may have been malevolently motivated to blame the random attack of a wild animal on an enemy disguised as a monster. The pictures here are not of werewolves, they're just plain wolves! And someday we'll wake up and notice that the better-lit nights of the full moon make it easier for humans to commit nocturnal crime, especially in the past where there was no street lighting.

THE WOLF OF THE WILD

Mankind has always had an uneasy relationship with the wolf. Some time in the distant past, a branch of the wolf family became 'man's best friend' but wolves, closely related to dogs, have remained fierce creatures. Although they are feared for hunting in packs, they would not attack humans unless provoked by them.

THE FRENCH WOLF

Thought to be a werewolf, the beast of Gévaudan terrorized the French countryside for three years between 1764 and 1767. Said to be the size of a cow, it claimed the lives of over 60 peasants by the time it was killed – shot in the chest by a silver bullet. Its stomach was said to contain the collar bone of a young woman, but its carcass was buried and has never been found.

ANCIENT WOLVES

Ancient writers talked of *lycanthropy*, *kuanthropy* and *boanthropy*, conditions of madness in which afflicted persons believed themselves to be a wolf, a dog, or a cow. In Northern Europe, similar tales were told of men who turned into bears, and in Africa, hyenas. The Greek historian Herodotus (*c.* 480-425 BC) claimed the Neuri people of Sarmatia (north-east Europe) were sorcerers: 'For each Neurian changes himself once a year into the form of a wolf, and continues in that form for several days, after which he resumes his former shape.'

BEAUTY & THE BEAST

The tale of a man who looks
(and often behaves) like an
animal is not limited
to werewolves.
It also crops up
in *The Strange Case
of Dr Jekyll and Mr Hyde*
(1886), and in the fairy tale of
Beauty and the Beast. The stories tell
of savage creatures who menace beautiful girls
– timeless representations of
mistrust between men
and women.

HAIRY MEN
OF MANDALAY

Don't believe humans can
get that hairy? A disease
called hypertrichosis can
cause excessive facial hair,
as in this photograph of
hairy men of Mandalay.
Since our distant ape
ancestors had hair
all over, it is only
relatively recently
in human history
that we began
to lose our
all-over
fur.

KALI

Kali, the Hindu Goddess of Death is one of the most fearsome creatures of mythology. Even today, animals are sacrificed to her, but in the past it was human beings who were offered to appease her anger. She is usually depicted as a black-skinned, red-eyed demon with four arms, wearing a necklace of skulls. The Indian city of Calcutta is said to derive from kali-ghat, the 'staircase of Kali' that her worshippers use to enter the River Ganges.

GARGOYLES

Originally simple spouts for draining water from the roofs of churches (French for gullet is *gargouille*), gargoyles were carved into a variety of grotesque stone demons. In the seventh century a great dragon called Gargouille was believed to live in the River Seine in Paris.

DEMONS & DEVILS

The Hindu *deva* and the Greek *daemon*, are both creatures of myth that have been changed over time into our words *devil* and *demon*. Once simple paranormal beings of both good and bad nature, they were proclaimed as wholly evil by the ascendence of Christianity. The Christian term *Satan* comes from the Hebrew word *shatana* which means *adversary*. In the Bible, Satan is identified in *Revelation* as meaning the same thing as the Dragon and the Serpent. In other words, the Devil. Satan is the supreme evil spirit, the enemy and tempter of man, and is the ruler of Hell.

PAN

Half man, half goat, the ancient Greek god Pan became a model for many Christian images of the devil. The cloven hooves and the horns especially seem to have been carried over into the modern idea of the Devil. We get our word panic from the terrible fear his appearance was intended to strike into non-believers.

FALLEN ANGELS

Biblical angels may do the bidding of God, but in the *Old Testament*, this often meant laying waste to armies, killing children and striking people down with diseases. John Milton linked this with the idea of Lucifer, and wrote the book *Paradise Lost*, a tale of Lucifer's expulsion from Heaven. The ousted angel and his followers prefer to be rulers in Hell than servants in Heaven.

LUCIFER

'How art thou fallen from Heaven, O Lucifer, star of the morning,' said the Bible's *Book of Isaiah*, poetically linking the death of the King of Babylon with the arrival of the morning star, Venus (*lucifer*: light-bringer). Over time, this phrase was confused with Satan himself, and the name Lucifer came to be identified with evil.

 FOOD FOR THOUGHT

What great stories. If people at war pretend their enemies are inhuman (to avoid admitting they are committing murder) the tales of ancient wars can fast become tales of demonic attacks. Like the fairies in earlier chapters, or the Sirens of ancient Greece, demons and devils are simply symbols of evil and temptation, perhaps even of past enemies. Blaming a devil for a wicked deed seems easier than taking responsibility for it.

VOODOO

Voodoo began in the beliefs of the African slaves of the 1800s, who were taken to work on French plantations in the New World. They believed sorcerers had the power to control zombies (the living dead). But zombies weren't really dead at all, they were people who had been fed a soup of the datura tree. It sedated them, slowing their heart-rate so they only appeared to be dead.

FOOD FOR THOUGHT

There's no arguing with Galvani's experiments. The same process is used to this day to jump-start failed hearts in hospital crash-carts. The Frankenstein story is rooted in a fear of science at a time when there were stories of doctors robbing graves so they could study the corpses. As for the restless dead, see the notes on vampires (pages 16-17). Modern-day afflictions such as schizophrenia or catatonia may have been interpreted in the past as possession by demons or living death. Kuru remains a fascinating topic for the modern scientist. Mad Cow Disease can pass to humans from eating the brains or spinal columns of infected cattle. Just think how much more dangerous the human variation must have been.

FRANKENSTEIN & THE LIVING DEAD

Many religions believe we all have a soul, and the human body is merely a vessel to carry around our consciousness. Myths about the afterlife often start with the question: what happens to someone when they die? The body may stop working but, so argue the religions, the soul goes somewhere else. A soul without a body is a ghost. So what is a body without a soul?

KURU

Cannibals of the South Pacific used to eat the brains of their enemies in order to gain their powers. Unfortunately, eating human flesh (especially brains) is liable to pass on some terrifying diseases, including kuru, the laughing sickness. The infected person went mad, supposedly possessed by evil spirits – another version of the living dead. And, once this enemy was defeated, the conquerors would eat his brain and catch the disease too.

GALVANI'S EXPERIMENTS

In 1791, the Italian scientist Luigi Galvani discovered that by passing electricity through the legs of a dead frog, he could make them twitch. It led to the supposition that electricity could bring the dead back to life. Because electricity seemed so mysterious, some people thought it must be the divine force that gave life to dead things.

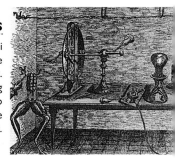

DAWN OF THE DEAD

Modern horror films take the zombie legends of other cultures and put a Christian spin on them. They claim that because Hell is full, some souls are waking up back in the bodies they are supposed to have left behind. Some films feature the zombies embarking on a quest for human brains, a strange craving that nevertheless recalls the kuru myths that partly inspired it.

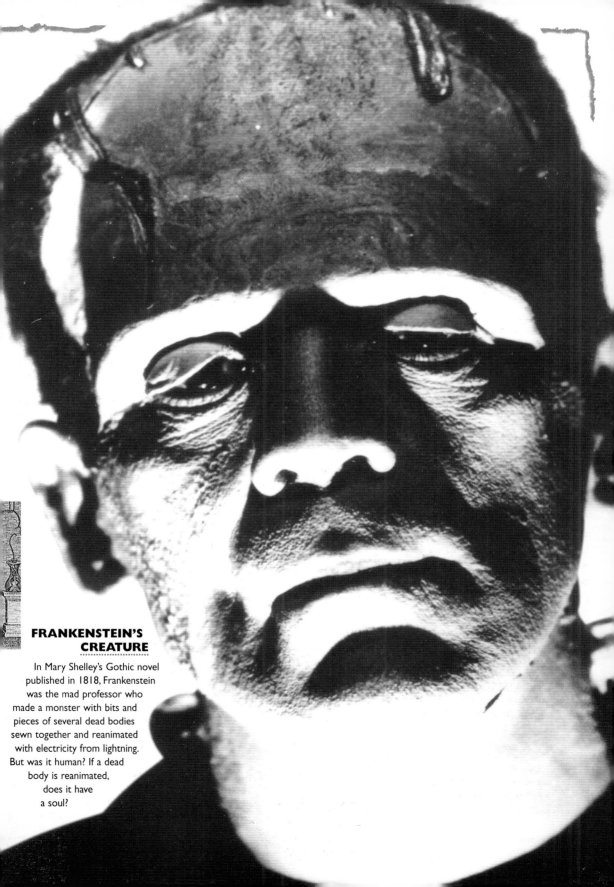

FRANKENSTEIN'S CREATURE

In Mary Shelley's Gothic novel
published in 1818, Frankenstein
was the mad professor who
made a monster with bits and
pieces of several dead bodies
sewn together and reanimated
with electricity from lightning.
But was it human? If a dead
body is reanimated,
does it have
a soul?

LAKE MONSTERS

Places as far afield as Sweden, Ireland, New Zealand, Africa, and Russia have their own mysterious monsters. In Iceland there is the Lágarfljótsormur, in the North American Lake Champlain there is Champ, and in Canada there is Manipogo, the monster of Lake Winnipeg. Far from being one of a kind, it would seem that Scotland's Loch Ness monster has many cousins around the world.

This convincing picture was taken on Loch Ness in 1977. But is it a monster's head or a branch?

NESSIE

Ever since AD 565, when Saint Columba ordered a creature in the loch to leave humans alone, the Loch Ness monster has been one of the most famous beasts of Scottish folklore. Often presumed to be a throwback to the time of the dinosaurs, Nessie is said to have either a long neck on a large body, or to be an eel-like shape, depending on who is telling the story.

Does Nessie have humps? This picture taken in 1951 by Lachlan Stuart would seem to suggest so. Or, are they just rocks?

FOOD FOR THOUGHT

Many of the lake-monster sightings have been discredited as hoaxes or proved to be something mundane like ducks, a swimming dog with a stick, or simply the wind blowing on the water. It is true that some prehistoric creatures may have survived in the vastness of the oceans, but the chances are remote of any remaining in the relatively tiny area of a lake. These things are not immortal; they would need others to breed with. There wouldn't be just one monster, but several per location. If they exist, surely we would have indisputable evidence by now.

OGOPOGO

In the Canadian province of British Columbia lies Lake Okanagan, where the native Okanakane Indians have always said there was a monster. They called him *Na-ha-ha-itkh*, and would throw a meat sacrifice into the lake whenever they crossed it. Known for its humps, its snakelike appearance and its thick body, Ogopogo is often sighted but has never harmed anyone in living memory. Ogopogo even had a song written about him in the 1920s: *His mother was an earwig, his father was a whale, a little bit of head, and hardly any tail, and Ogopogo was his name.*

ISSIE

This is a model of Issie, the monster rumoured to live in the depths of Lake Ikeda in Japan. Like Nessie, it has never been known to harm humans and seems to be very camera shy. Though many people have *almost* photographed it, a conclusive picture has yet to appear.

LAKE IKEDA, JAPAN

A lake just waiting for a monster. This inexplicable ripple could mean Issie is about to surface.

SEA MONSTERS

TEMPEST

As late as the Elizabethan era (1558-1603), large areas of the globe remained uncharted. When Shakespeare wrote *The Tempest*, he was inspired by tales of monsters and shipwrecks that had circulated from the New World (the Americas). For the people of pre-modern times, monsters such as this were thought to be lurking just outside mapped areas. Any journey was a journey into the unknown, and into fear.

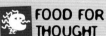 **FOOD FOR THOUGHT**

The thought of a whale shark is very scary, but it isn't a monster. Neither is a shark. We invade their territory, not the other way around. The whales and sharks of ancient tales probably grew in the telling to give us the sea monsters of yore, but there's no arguing with some of the evidence. Nine-metre (30 ft) squid have been found and studied by scientists and, if the scars on the sperm whales are anything to go by, they could well be the babies. No one knows how big a full-grown giant squid might be.

Two-thirds of the Earth is covered by water. Although we know most of the land well there are still unexplored areas of the deep sea that remain a mystery. History is rich with stories of sea monsters. Sailors told tales of many extraordinary creatures, such as the now legendary mercreatures who were said to have the body of a human and the tail of a fish. What the sailors had seen were probably dolphins, narwhals, or dugongs. Perhaps they had been at sea too long or had had an extra tipple of rum before going on watch. But not all the sightings were quite so fanciful. Until 1938, coelocanths were thought to have become extinct some 50 million years ago. It is now known that a small number of coelocanths live in very deep water off the African coast. If *they* have survived for millions of years, other prehistoric 'monsters', such as the megalodon, a 30-metre (100-ft) shark, may also still be cruising about in the unexplored depths of some ocean.

FANGTOOTH

This scary-looking fish is actually quite small, and unlikely to turn up anywhere near people because it lives miles down in the sea. On the rare occasions when it is washed up on shore, such teeth might scare humans into imagining what a giant version would look like.

OCTOPI

The octopus has always intrigued seafarers. With its eight arms, its suckers and its powerful hidden beak, it is one of the strangest creatures of the deep. As stories grow with the telling, many have speculated on the existence of giant octopi large enough to swallow a man whole.

GIANT SQUID

Thought to be the stuff of legend, the giant squid (or kraken) may well exist. The first people to discuss it were the crews of the whaling ships in the nineteenth century. Some whales they killed had the scars of giant suckers on them, as if they had survived a battle. F.T. Bullen reported a harpooned sperm whale vomiting thousands of squid (its traditional diet). Also among the detritus were huge bits of tentacle as thick as a man's body. This nineteenth century Japanese print shows a giant squid as one of the legendary Dragon King's faithful army.

WHALES

The great size of whales has always struck dread into the hearts of sailors, but these peaceful creatures have no interest in harming humanity. Their value as food and for raw materials in candles and corsets (among other things) meant that they have been hunted to the brink of extinction. But whales must have been terrifying for early whalers who had nothing but spears to throw.

SHARKS

Sharks are our modern-day sea monsters, but not because sharks are evil (although, like this blue shark, some do look evil). Unless provoked, most sharks will leave humans alone. The biggest known fish in the world is the whale shark – a huge 18 metres (60 ft) long, but it doesn't eat people, just tiny plant and animal organisms called plankton.

THE YETI

The Abominable Snowman, or Yeti, is perhaps
the most famous ape-like creature. It may be
a distant, ape-like, relative of man. The people
of the Himalayas believe it exists, and the
mountain range is so remote it is possible that
undiscovered creatures do live there. In 1975, a
Polish hiker called Janusz Tomaszczuk claimed
he had been approached by an ape-like creature
in the Himalayas. His screams drove it away.

THE SCOTTISH SNOWMAN

This photograph
was taken high up
on Ben Nevis, the
highest mountain in
the British Isles. Is it
the Scottish equivalent
of the Yeti? Or just a
man in a gorilla suit?

YETI'S FOOTPRINTS

Nobody has ever captured
a Yeti, but its footprints
have been photographed.
These deep, large footprints
are spaced wide apart and
suggest a tall, heavy
creature. It certainly isn't
human. But it might be the
elusive Tibetan blue bear, a
creature that has not been
seen alive by Westerners
but whose skins have been
sold to museums.

GREAT APES

Like the werewolf, what scares us most about the great apes is how like and yet how different they are to us. The gentlest of the great apes, the mountain gorilla, was regarded as a fanciful invention of storytellers until the early years of the twentieth century. Perhaps the stories of the Himalayan Yeti, the American Big Foot or the Russian Alma are equally well founded.

KING KONG

A classic horror film tells the tale of King Kong, a 15-metre (50-ft) prehistoric great ape (the eighth wonder of the world) who is captured, taken to New York and put on display. He escapes and terrorizes the city before finally falling to his death from the Empire State Building. His climactic rampage through the city was the result of human intervention, which made his death all the more tragic.

BIG FEET

If this 1995 Big Foot photograph is a fake it means someone has been crazy enough to make false Big Foot tracks running for several miles in remote parts of the US and Canada.

🦎 FOOD FOR THOUGHT

There may yet be more creatures for us to discover in the wilderness. The existence of a Scottish apeman is doubtful, but Canada and the Himalayas are large enough to allow for the possibility of undiscovered life. Since mountain gorillas exist, there's a chance that the Yeti could too. Or perhaps Big Foot? Both these great apes are reputed to live in wastelands devoid of human habitation and would probably be more scared of us than we are of them.

BIG FOOT

In 1967, Roger Patterson took this famous film of an ape-like figure in Northern California. Its height is estimated at 2 metres (6 ft 5 in). Could *Pithecanthropus Erectus*, a species of primitive man believed to be extinct, still live in remote parts of the world?

MODERN MONSTERS

MINI-MONSTERS

Just as our forebears feared the 'little people', we have something tiny of our own to worry about. Our improved scientific understanding of what causes diseases has given us something very real to fear. We now know that under a microscope we can see scarier creatures than we could ever imagine – viruses, bacteria, and other tiny disease-carrying organisms. Even the ordinary head louse above looks monstrous.

Although we like to think we are less gullible than our ancestors, modern people find just as many things to be afraid of. But the monsters that scare us today are no longer dragons in the sea or goblins in the forests. We live in a scientific, technological age which creates its own monsters. The instinct to feel fear is part of our heritage. It may keep us awake at night or send shivers down our spine, but it also alerts us to look both ways when we cross the road, or to stay away from dangerous animals and situations. Dragons, giants and goblins may have disappeared into the story-books, but that doesn't mean there is nothing to be afraid of. In modern times, there are more monsters than ever.

 ## FOOD FOR THOUGHT

Science can explain the dark and the animalistic, but it can't stop people being afraid. There will always be things we do not understand. Everything we learn uncovers another mystery, another monster, another scary story. Modern monsters are not born out of superstition or religious beliefs, but out of science and technology. We can see the tiny monsters that make us ill; we imagine the terror of machinery gone mad, a world poisoned, or a bomb to end all bombs. As long as there are stories to tell, so there will be monsters to fear.

IRRATIONAL FEARS

Today, we are better educated and more worldly-wise than our ancestors but that doesn't stop us finding plenty to feel afraid of. Intense irrational fears are called phobias of which there are many, including: claustrophobia, a fear of enclosed spaces; acrophobia, a dread of heights; agoraphobia, a fear of open spaces; arachnophobia, a fear of spiders. We know perfectly well that most spiders are harmless, yet many people are terrified of them all. Some people are even afraid of moths. So it seems monsters are still the product of our own minds.

THE ATOM

The atom is one of the tiniest building blocks of the universe, and the discovery that we could split it has unleashed one of the most devastating weapons known to man. Nuclear weapons are now *the* most terrifyingly destructive monsters of the modern world.

ALIENS

Even though almost every inch of the Earth has been mapped and millions of its creatures chronicled, some believe that there may be aliens out there somewhere – and if not already here, then on their way. Invasion and abduction by aliens are popular themes in science fiction stories. It is almost as if we have a real need for an external enemy on whom to focus our fears.

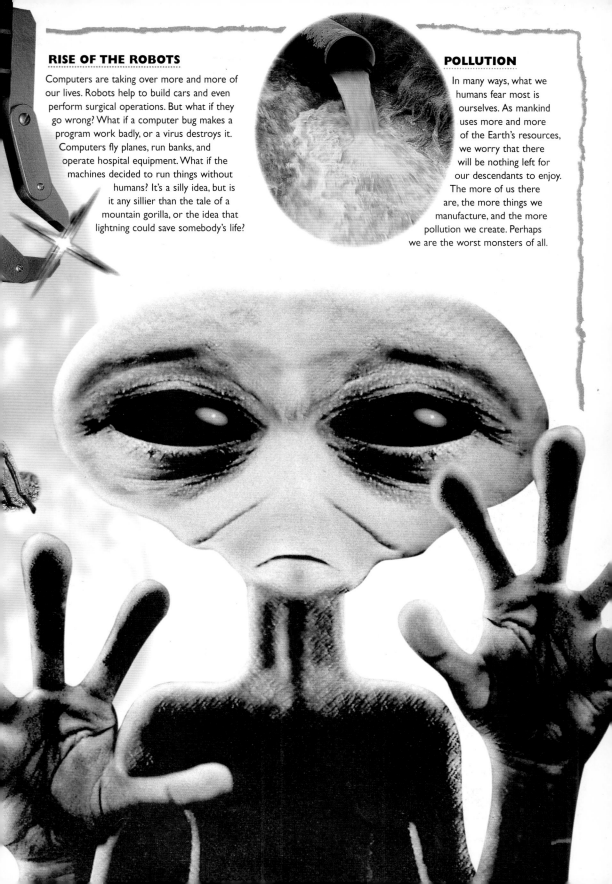

RISE OF THE ROBOTS

Computers are taking over more and more of our lives. Robots help to build cars and even perform surgical operations. But what if they go wrong? What if a computer bug makes a program work badly, or a virus destroys it. Computers fly planes, run banks, and operate hospital equipment. What if the machines decided to run things without humans? It's a silly idea, but is it any sillier than the tale of a mountain gorilla, or the idea that lightning could save somebody's life?

POLLUTION

In many ways, what we humans fear most is ourselves. As mankind uses more and more of the Earth's resources, we worry that there will be nothing left for our descendants to enjoy. The more of us there are, the more things we manufacture, and the more pollution we create. Perhaps we are the worst monsters of all.